FOLENS IDEAS BANK MATHEMATICS

Multiplying and Dividing

David Kirkby

Contents

How to use this book	2	Multiplying by 9	26
Introduction	3	Hundred Game	28
Choc Boxes	4	Remainder Athletics	30
Multiplication Tables	6	The Factor Tribe	32
Counting Squares	8	Make it Big!	34
Dragons	10	Number Machine	36
Multiplying by 3	12	Prime Time	38
Multiple Patterns	14	Multiple Cards	40
Multiplication Tables	16	Homework Marking	42
Multiplication Monsters	18	Line Graphs	44
Bingo	20	Calculator Division	46
Racing Cars	22	Eight ways to help ...	48
Cat, Rabbit or Koala	24		

How to use this book

Ideas Bank books provide you with ready to use, practical photocopiable activity pages for your children **plus** a wealth of ideas for extension and development.

Clear focus to the activity. — TEACHER IDEAS PAGE

Suggestions for developing work on the photocopiable pages.

Ideas for maths display in the classroom

PHOTOCOPIABLE ACTIVITY PAGE

Extension activities suggested to take the work one step further.

Independent activities for children to work with.

- Time saving, relevant and practical, **Ideas Bank** books ensure that you will always have work ready at hand.

Folens books are protected by international copyright laws. All rights reserved. The copyright of all materials in this book, except where otherwise stated, remains the property of the publisher and author(s). No part of this publication may be reproduced, stored in a retrieval system, or transmitted, in any form or by any means, for whatever purpose, without the written permission of Folens Limited.

Folens do allow photocopying of selected pages of this publication for educational use, providing that this use is within the confines of the purchasing institution. You may make as many copies as you require for classroom use of the pages so marked.
This resource may be used in a variety of ways; however it is not intended that teachers or students should write into the book itself.

© 1993 Folens Limited, on behalf of the author.

Cover by: In Touch Creative Services Ltd.   Cover photo: Pierre-Yves Goavec (The Image Bank)

Illustrations by: Chris Roper

First published 1993 by Folens Limited, Albert House, Apex Business Centre, Boscombe Road, Dunstable, LU5 4RL, England.

ISBN 1 85276534-8

Printed by Ashford Colour Press

© 1993 Folens Ltd.

Introduction

The nature of the resource

This resource contains twenty two activities on the theme of Multiplying and Dividing. Although most of the activities are appropriate for children at Key Stage 2, some of them will be appropriate for use at Key Stage 3. Each activity contains a photocopiable page for classroom use, together with a page of teacher notes to illustrate ways in which the activity page can be used.

Particular ingredients of this resource include:

- emphasis on the use of materials to support the children's learning
- fostering an investigational approach to learning mathematics
- the use of games as an integral part of the learning experience
- importance of display to support and extend the activities
- encouragement of the inclusion of mental mathematics alongside the activities.

The activity pages

These are photocopiable and serve various purposes:

- sheets to be completed by the children
- tables and grids to be coloured and shaded
- boards and scoresheets for mathematical games
- pictures to be used with other pieces of apparatus
- pages to be photocopied on to card, which are then cut up to produce sets of cards for children to use in activities
- mock completed mathematical exercises for the children to mark.

The activities

These are varied in type, and cover a range of learning experiences in multiplication and division. It is desirable that children receive a varied diet of mathematical activity. This particular diet includes:

- games
- apparatus based activities
- investigational activities, and the search for pattern
- practical activities.

The activities are not presented sequentially, leaving teachers to choose particular pages as appropriate. Each activity is capable of extension and variation in different ways. Several relevant suggestions are made on the appropriate Ideas page.

The Ideas pages

These include comments and suggestions to help the teacher make full use of the activity pages. In particular:

- purpose of the activity
- descriptions of activities which use the photocopiable apparatus, e.g. cards
- solutions where necessary
- rules for the games, with variations
- ideas for display
- extension ideas
- relevant mental activities.

Choc Boxes - Ideas Page

Aims

- To develop an understanding of the concept of multiplication.
- To illustrate the commutative law.

Activities

Activity page

The cards can be photocopied on to card, coloured and then cut out. Laminate them for longer life!

Ask the children to:
- Use the Monster Multiplication cards on page 19 to match, where possible, the appropriate multiplication sum to the chocolate box card.
- Arrange counters or sweets to copy the arrangement on a particular card.
- Look at a card and count
  - the number of rows
  - the number of columns
  - the number of chocolates.
- Sort the cards into sets according to the number of rows, i.e. chocolates arranged in two rows, three rows, four rows, five rows.
- Sort the cards according to the number of columns, i.e. chocolates arranged in two, three, four, five and six columns.

Paired activity

- One child turns over a card and says the number of rows and the number of columns. The other child says the number of chocolates.
- This activity can be reversed so that the child counts, then says, the number of chocolates on the card. The other child tries to guess the number of rows and columns.

The commutative law

- Pair the cards if they have equal numbers of chocolates, e.g.

This will help to consolidate the commutative law for multiplication, e.g.

2 x 4 = 4 x 2 = 8.

Display

Children can stick the cards on to backing sheets and write the multiplications:

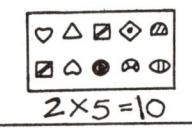

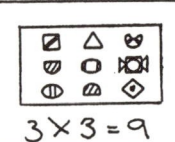

They can use pegs in pegboards to create different rectangular arrangements:

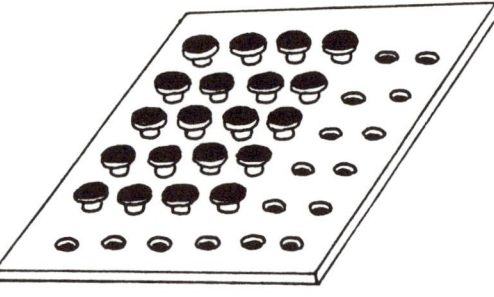

Extension

- Provide children with a set of counters. Invite them to take twelve counters, and arrange them into rows and columns.
- Discuss different ways of doing this:

```
oooo    oooooo    oo
oooo              oo
oooo      ooo     oo
          ooo     oo
          ooo     oo
          ooo     oo
```

- Try with different numbers of counters. What happens with thirteen counters, or seven counters?

Choc Boxes

- The cards show different arrangements of chocolates.
- Cut out the cards and sort them.

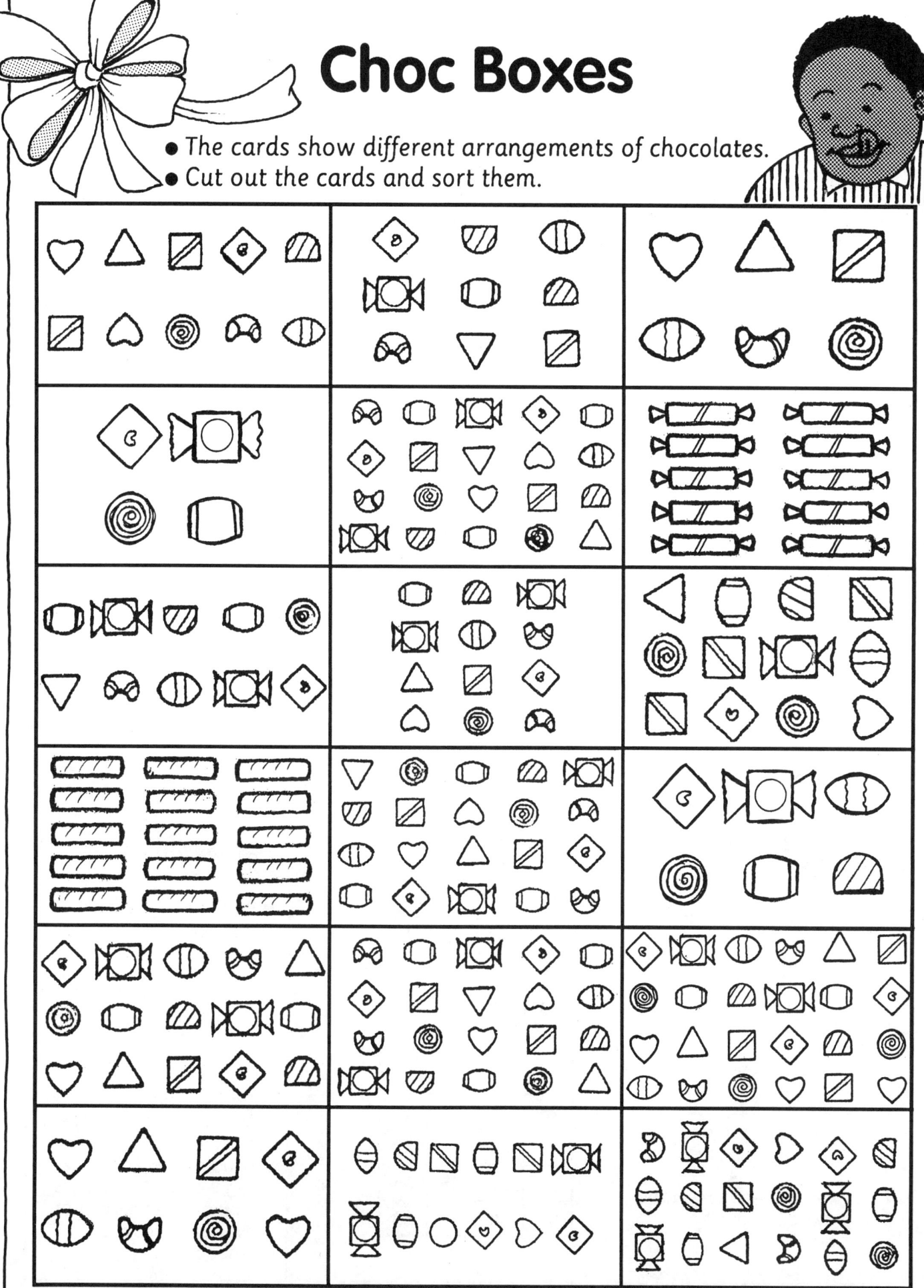

Multiplication Tables - Ideas Page

Aims

- To create the multiples of different numbers, leading towards learning multiplication facts.
- To explore patterns in the multiples.

Activities

Creative writing

Ask the children to:
- Choose a number from two to nine. The multiples of their number are a family.
- Describe the members of their family:
  - Who is the youngest?
  - Who is the eldest?
  - What do the members of your family have in common?
  - What do they look like?
  - What shape are they?
- Describe what happens when they meet another family.

Mental mathematics

Invite the children to:
- Recite the multiples of different numbers, without looking at the table, extending beyond the tenth multiple.
- Recite the multiples backwards, starting at the tenth multiple.
- Imagine the multiples of e.g. four, and answer questions like:
  - Which number is at the end of the fifth row?
  - Which row contains twenty four?
  - Which number is below twelve?
  - Which is above thirty six?

Activity page

- Ask the children to complete each table by writing numbers in order from left to right.
- The multiples for each table are highlighted.
- The children could keep the tables in their maths books or files and use them for games or checking their own work.

Display

Enlarge the grids opposite on the photocopier for display. Write numbers in order from left to right and use a bright colour to highlight the multiples in the right-hand column.
These can be used to consolidate understanding of the multiples, their patterns, multiplication facts and associated division facts.

Squared paper can be used to draw tables of other multiples.

1	2	3	4
5	6	7	8
9	10	11	12
13	14	15	16
17	18	19	20
21	22	23	24
25	26	27	28
29	30	31	32
33	34	35	36
37	38	39	40

Extension

- Extend the grids beyond the tenth row to consider further multiples.
- Investigate the multiples of numbers which are:
  - all odd
  - all even
  - a mixture of odd and even.
- Explore patterns in the last digits of the multiples.
- Draw new grids on squared paper with six, eight and nine columns, to show the multiples of six, eight and nine respectively.

© 1993 Folens Ltd.

Multiplication Tables

● Complete each table by writing numbers in order from left to right.

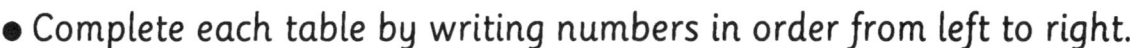

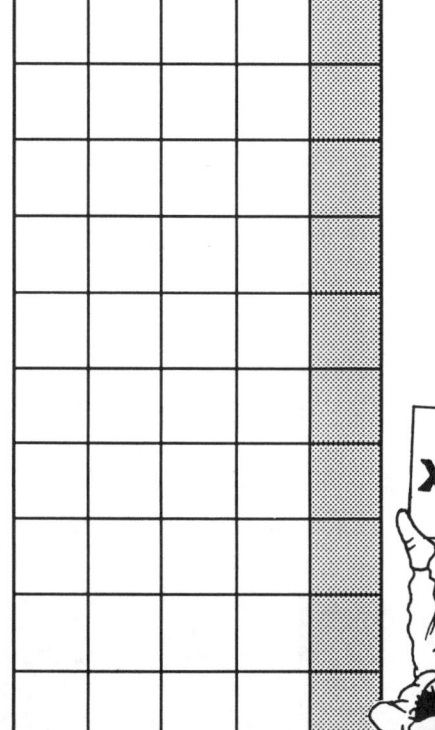
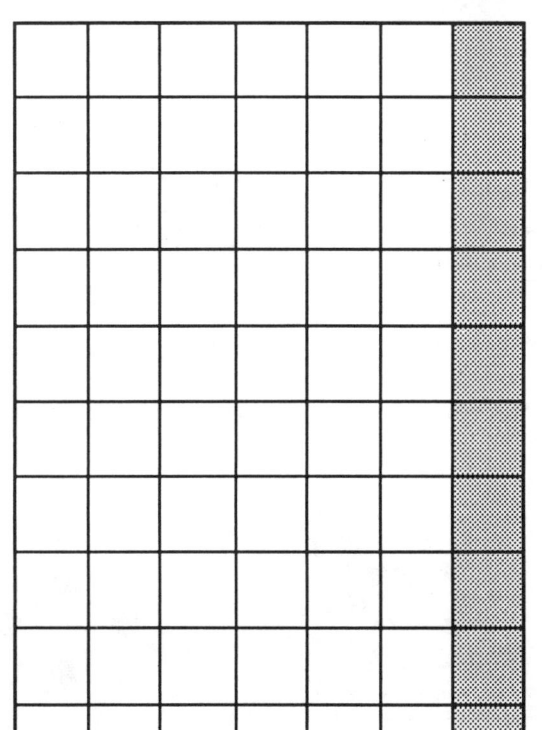

Counting Squares - Ideas Page

Aims

- To introduce multiplication as repeated addition.
- To illustrate the commutative law, i.e. a x b = b x a.

Activities

More squares

After completing the activity sheet opposite, invite the children to cut up squared paper to illustrate multiplication facts.
- Are there different shaped cut-outs which have the same number in the corner?
  e.g.

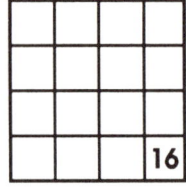
4 x 4 = 16

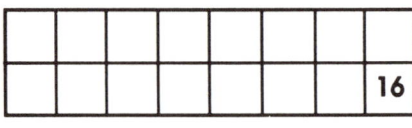
2 x 8 = 16

- How many others can be found?
- Find examples to show the commutative law:

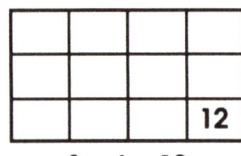
3 x 4 = 12

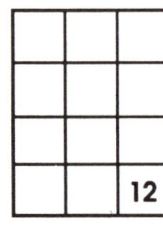
4 x 3 = 12

Mental mathematics

- If there are three rows of four, how many tiles?
- How many tiles in two rows of five, three rows of five, four rows of five, ...?
- If there are twelve tiles, how many rows can there be?

Display

Many examples exist to illustrate rows of objects. You could display:

Tiles on the wall

Milk bottles in a crate

Eggs in a box

Further illustrations of rows of objects to model multiplication include:

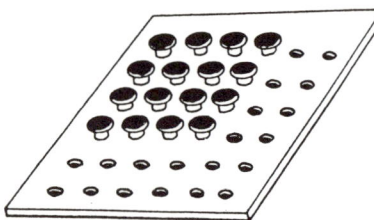
Pegs in a pegboard

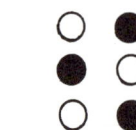 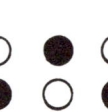
Arranging counters

Extension

- Build up a multiplication square using the results of the activites above:

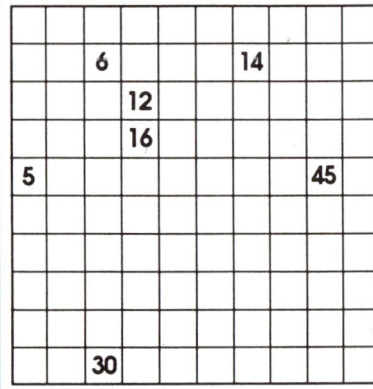

- Investigate which numbers up to one hundred do not appear in the multiplication square.
- Investigate numbers which appear several times, and which numbers appear most often.

© 1993 Folens Ltd.

Counting Squares

- These mats are made from square tiles.

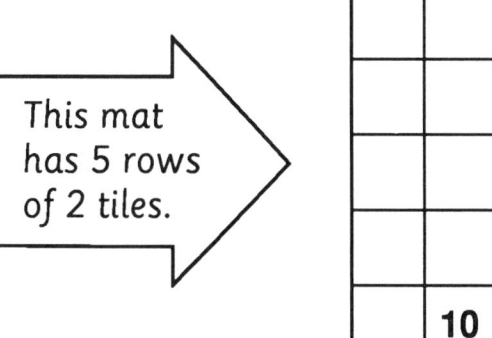

This mat has 5 rows of 2 tiles.

10

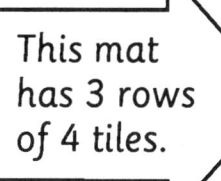

This mat has 3 rows of 4 tiles.

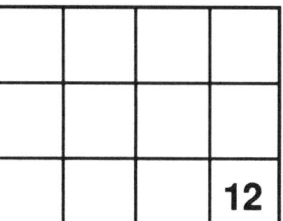

12

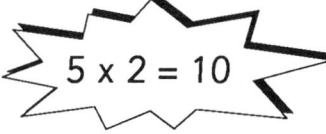

5 x 2 = 10

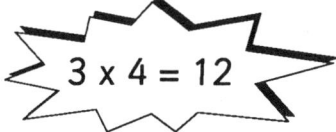

3 x 4 = 12

- Complete these mats by writing the number of tiles in the corner, and the multiplication in the stars underneath them.

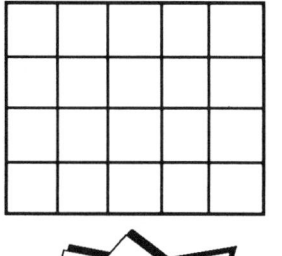

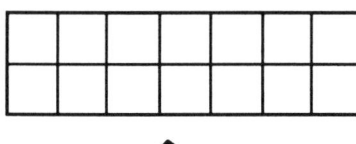

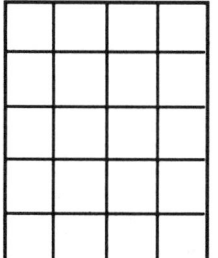

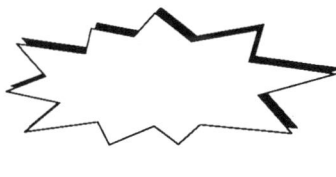

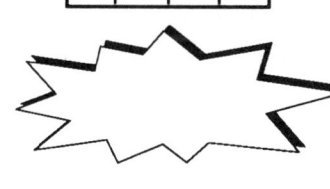

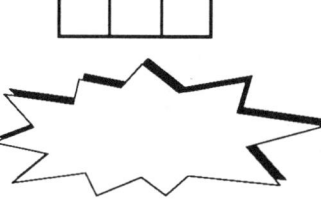

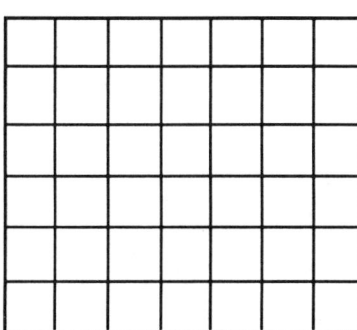

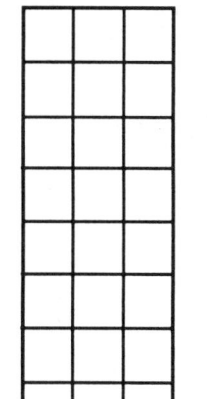

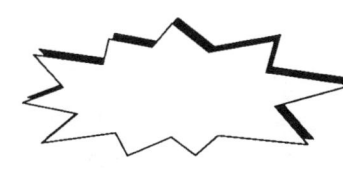

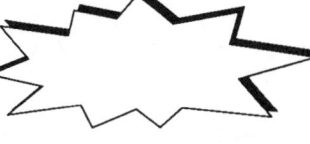

Dragons - Ideas Page

Aim

- To practise learning division facts.

Activity page

The dragon cards can be photocopied on to card, coloured and then cut out. Laminate them for longer life.

Sorting the dragons

- Sort the cards, in order, in a line, smallest on the left, largest on the right.
- Sort the cards into two sets: odd-numbered answers and even-numbered answers.
- There are three dragons, each with answers three, four, five, six, seven and eight.

3	6 ÷ 2	9 ÷ 3	12 ÷ 4
4	20 ÷ 5	24 ÷ 6	8 ÷ 2
5	15 ÷ 3	35 ÷ 7	40 ÷ 8
6	12 ÷ 2	24 ÷ 4	30 ÷ 5
7	49 ÷ 7	21 ÷ 3	42 ÷ 6
8	32 ÷ 4	6 ÷ 2	40 ÷ 5

Activities

Dragon game 1 *For two players*

- Spread the cards face down on the table.
- Each player chooses one card and turns it over.
- The player whose card has the largest answer wins the trick and collects both cards.
- If both cards have the same value, then each player keeps one card.
- Continue until all cards have been collected.
- The winner is the player who has collected the most cards.

Dragon game 2 *For two or more players*

- Make a dice numbered three to eight.
- Shuffle the cards and deal them out to each player.
- Each player takes it in turn to throw the dice. If their card has an answer to match the dice score the player can place it in front of him/her.
- Continue taking turns, and placing cards.
- The winner is the first player to reveal all cards.

Dragon game 3 *For two or more players*

- Spread the cards, face down, on the table.
- Take turns to turn over any two cards allowing each player to see. If they have the same value the player takes both cards and turns over a second pair, and so on. If they do not have the same value s/he replaces them face down in their original position on the table. The next player then has his/her chance and the game continues.
- The winner is the player with the most cards when all have been removed from the table.

Display

- Make a display showing '6-dragons', i.e. division facts which produce an answer of six.

- Extend to other division facts.

Extension

- Write the answers on the back of the dragon cards.
- Place the cards in a pile, face up. The children can take them one at a time, say the answer and check it on the back.
- The correctly answered cards should be placed in a pile to the right and the incorrect ones to the left.
- Can the children avoid placing any cards to the left?

© 1993 Folens Ltd.

Dragons

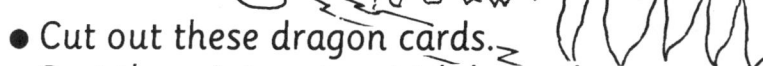

- Cut out these dragon cards.
- Sort them into sets which have the same answer.

6 ÷ 2	21 ÷ 3	20 ÷ 5
15 ÷ 3	12 ÷ 2	24 ÷ 4
30 ÷ 5	40 ÷ 5	8 ÷ 2
40 ÷ 8	9 ÷ 3	49 ÷ 7
42 ÷ 6	24 ÷ 6	16 ÷ 2
12 ÷ 4	32 ÷ 4	35 ÷ 7

Multiplying by 3 - Ideas Page

Aim

- To consolidate the concept of multiplying by three.

Activities

More jugglers

- Ask the children to draw pictures of the jugglers opposite and their associated multiplication facts, e.g.

 1 juggler   1 × 3 = 3 balls

 2 jugglers   2 × 3 = 6 balls

 3 jugglers   3 × 3 = 9 balls

Mental mathematics

- How many balls have three jugglers got?
- If there are fifteen balls, how many jugglers are there?

Ask the children to imagine the 'end' numbers in the three times table.

- Which number comes below the nine?
- Which number comes above the eighteen?
- What is the seventh number?
- Recite the multiples of three in order.
- Recite them backwards from thirty.

Display

The jugglers could be displayed to show the three times table. Make another display of animals with different numbers of legs to show other multiplication facts:

 3 birds 3 × 2 = 6 legs

 3 dogs 3 × 4 = 12 legs

 2 octopuses 2 × 8 = 16 legs

The children could invent creatures with five, seven or nine legs and draw them for a similar multiplication facts display.

Extension

- Consider other objects based on three, e.g. wheels of tricycles, sides of triangles.

 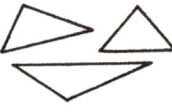

- Build towers of three with interlocking cubes.

- Use counters to build rows of three, or use pegs in a pegboard.

© 1993 Folens Ltd.

Multiplying by 3

- Each juggler has 3 balls.
- Draw the missing balls above each juggler.

Complete these tables.

Number of jugglers	Total balls
1	1 x 3 = 3
2	2 x 3 = 6
3	
4	
5	
6	
7	
8	
9	
10	

Write the numbers in order from left to right.

1	2	3
4	5	6
7		

NOW

Complete this table.

3 x table										
Digit sum										

- What do you notice about the digit sums

Multiple Patterns – Ideas Page

Aim

- To explore patterns in the multiples of different numbers.

Activities

x2, **x3**, **x4**, **x5**, **x6**, **x7**, **x8**, **x9**

Activity page

- Some multiples give chequered patterns, some column patterns, some diagonal patterns.

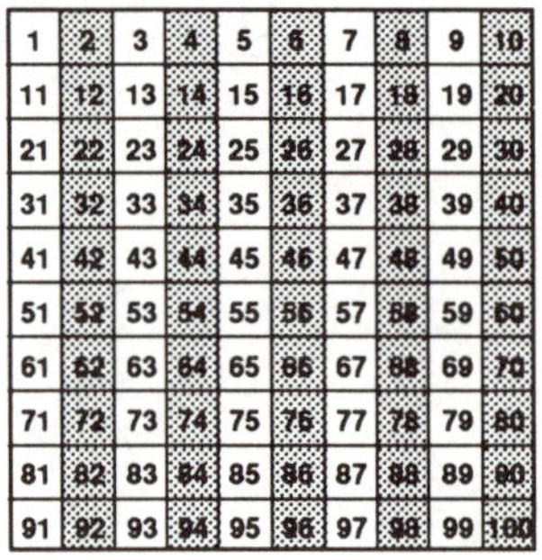

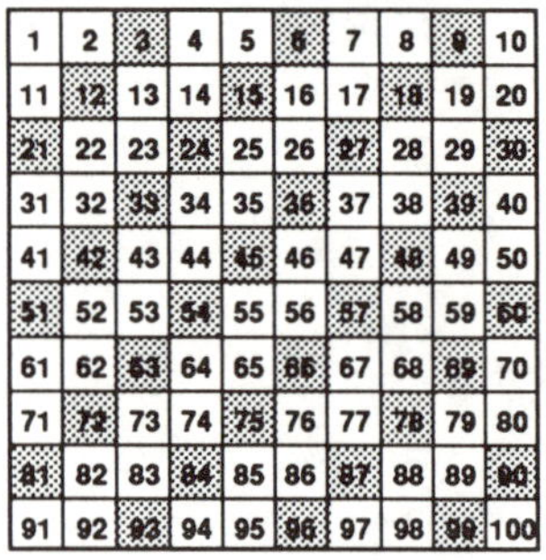

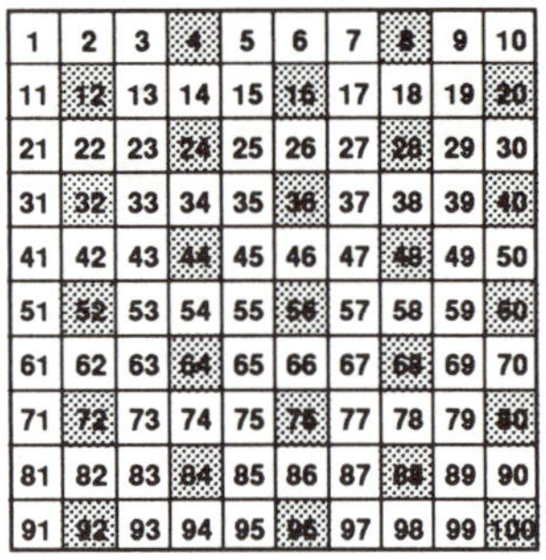

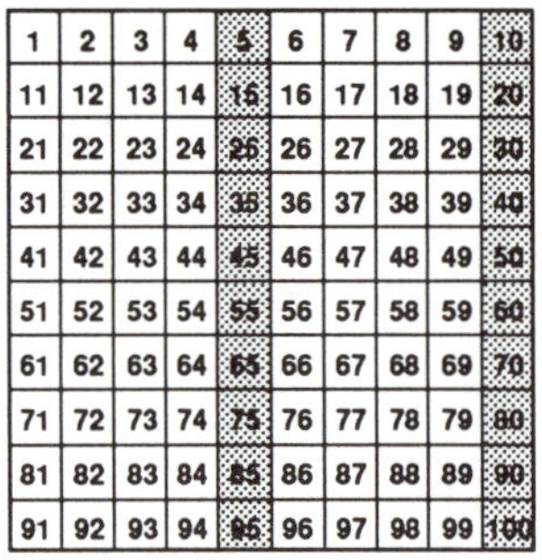

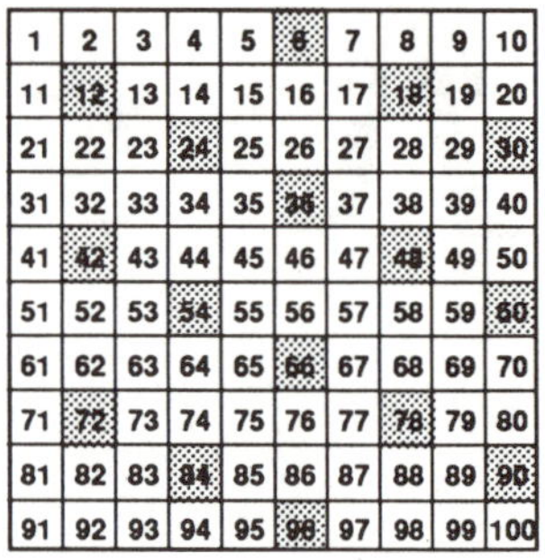

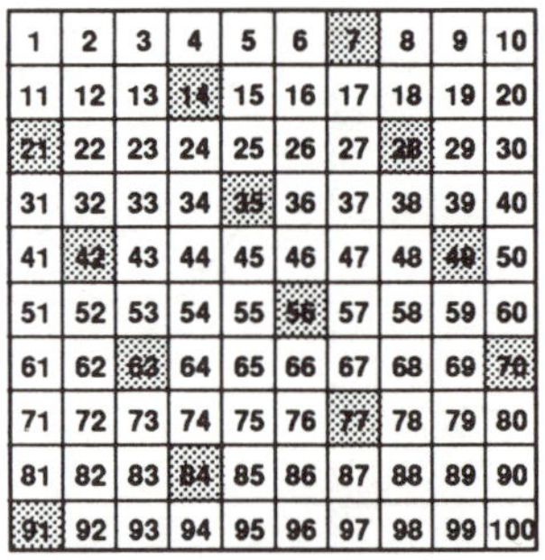

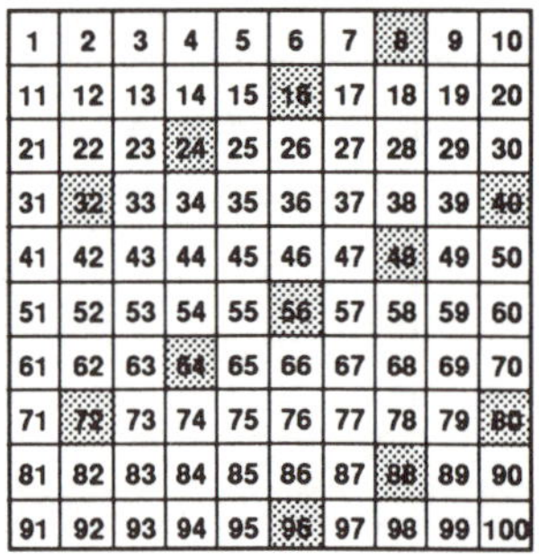

Display

Make masks by cutting out holes from squares drawn on card. The masks can then be placed over a one hundred number square on the wall to highlight the multiples:

X 2, **X 3**

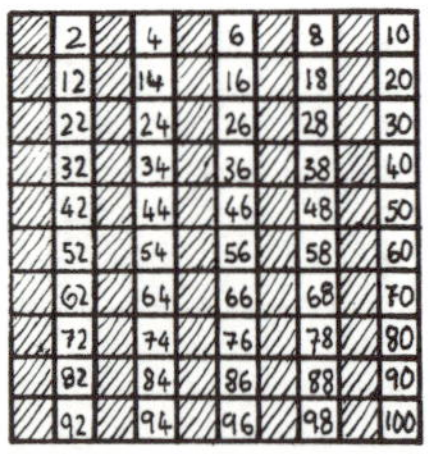

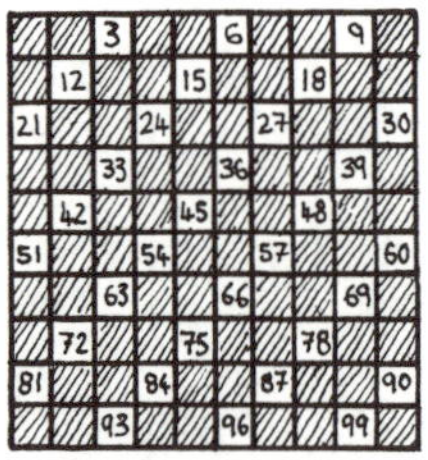

Two masks can be superimposed on top of each other to illustrate common multiples of two numbers.

Extension

- Draw a large one hundred square on the floor or playground.
- Place hoops on the squares to highlight patterns.
- The children can also stand on the squares to make patterns.
- Investigate patterns in the sums of the digits of the numbers on each coloured square, for a particular multiple. E.g. with the multiples of nine, then the sums of the digits are nine.

© 1993 Folens Ltd.

Multiple Patterns

Use each 100 square to colour the multiples of a number. Look for and describe the patterns in the coloured squares.

Multiples of 3

1	2	3	4	5	6	7	8	9	10
11	12	13	14	15	16	17	18	19	20
21	22	23	24	25	26	27	28	29	30
31	32	33	34	35	36	37	38	39	40
41	42	43	44	45	46	47	48	49	50
51	52	53	54	55	56	57	58	59	60
61	62	63	64	65	66	67	68	69	70
71	72	73	74	75	76	77	78	79	80
81	82	83	84	85	86	87	88	89	90
91	92	93	94	95	96	97	98	99	100

Multiples of 4

1	2	3	4	5	6	7	8	9	10
11	12	13	14	15	16	17	18	19	20
21	22	23	24	25	26	27	28	29	30
31	32	33	34	35	36	37	38	39	40
41	42	43	44	45	46	47	48	49	50
51	52	53	54	55	56	57	58	59	60
61	62	63	64	65	66	67	68	69	70
71	72	73	74	75	76	77	78	79	80
81	82	83	84	85	86	87	88	89	90
91	92	93	94	95	96	97	98	99	100

Multiples of 5

1	2	3	4	5	6	7	8	9	10
11	12	13	14	15	16	17	18	19	20
21	22	23	24	25	26	27	28	29	30
31	32	33	34	35	36	37	38	39	40
41	42	43	44	45	46	47	48	49	50
51	52	53	54	55	56	57	58	59	60
61	62	63	64	65	66	67	68	69	70
71	72	73	74	75	76	77	78	79	80
81	82	83	84	85	86	87	88	89	90
91	92	93	94	95	96	97	98	99	100

Multiples of 6

1	2	3	4	5	6	7	8	9	10
11	12	13	14	15	16	17	18	19	20
21	22	23	24	25	26	27	28	29	30
31	32	33	34	35	36	37	38	39	40
41	42	43	44	45	46	47	48	49	50
51	52	53	54	55	56	57	58	59	60
61	62	63	64	65	66	67	68	69	70
71	72	73	74	75	76	77	78	79	80
81	82	83	84	85	86	87	88	89	90
91	92	93	94	95	96	97	98	99	100

 • Colour the patterns of other multiples.

Multiplication Tables - Ideas Page

Aims

- To consolidate table facts for the multiples of one to five.
- To build up a multiplication square.

Mental mathematics

- What number ball is below eighteen and above sixteen on the six times seal?
- Recite the numbers of the balls balanced by the four times seal, upwards and downwards.
- Which seals will be balancing a ball numbered six, a ball numbered four, and so on?

Activities

Activity page

After filling in the missing numbers, ask the children to investigate the numbers on the balls:

- Which numbers occur only once?
- Which numbers occur more than once?
- Which number appears most often?
- Which numbers do not occur at all?

Multiples six to ten

The children could draw their own seals to show multiples six to ten.

Display

Make a seal colony multiplication table for the wall using sticky circles for each ball:

Extension

- Colour the odd-numbered balls yellow, and the even numbered balls blue.
- Discuss the resulting pattern, i.e:
  - multiples of two, four, six, eight and ten are all even
  - multiples of one, three, five, seven and nine alternate between odd and even.
- Discuss the numbering of the balls if each seal could balance more balls, e.g. fifteen altogether, then twenty altogether.
- Discuss the units digits of the balls balanced by each seal in turn.

© 1993 Folens Ltd.

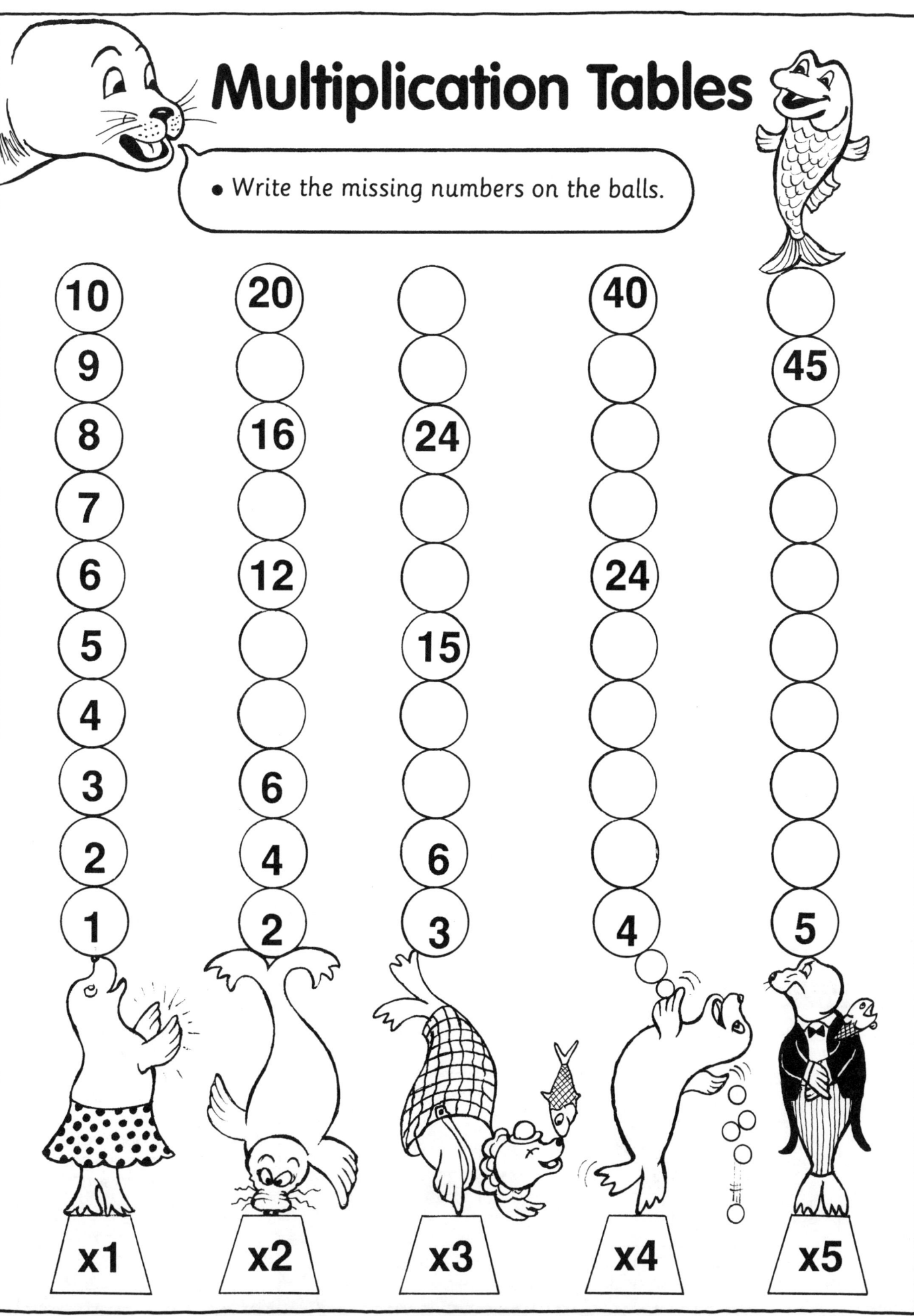

Multiplication Monsters - Ideas Page

Aim

- To consolidate the learning of multiplication facts up to six times six.

Activities

Flash cards

- Use the cards as flash cards.
- Children could work on their own, in pairs or with an adult.
- Shuffle the cards and place them in a pile.
- Turn them over one at time.
- The children should attempt to say the product each time.

Monster card game   *For two players*

- Deal the cards out equally, into two piles, face down.
- Each player reveals their top card. The player with the highest product collects both cards and puts them to one side.
- Players continue to reveal top cards until they have all been turned over.
- The winner is the player who has collected most cards.
  (At each stage both players should discuss the answer to each card.)

Variation

Instead of collecting cards, points are tallied. The player with the highest product scores points according to the difference in answers:

Activity page

The cards can be photocopied on to card, coloured and then cut out. Laminate them for longer life.

- The order of the monster cards (from smallest to largest size of product):

- Which monsters have the same answer?
- Which monster has the largest/smallest product?

Display

The cards can be sorted into even and odd monsters and displayed on the wall:

The children should notice that odd x odd = odd, odd x even = even, even x even = even and even x odd = even.

Extension

- The children could make their own monster multiplication cards based on numbers greater than six.
- They could also make matching answer cards for a partner to sort:

 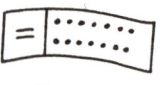

© 1993 Folens Ltd.

Multiplication Monsters

- Cut out these monster cards.
- Arrange them in a line with the smallest answer on the left and the largest answer on the right.

Bingo - Ideas Page

Aim

- To practise the learning of multiplication facts.

Activity page

The cards can be photocopied on to card and then cut out. Laminate them for longer life.

- The children can work in groups of three to play the bingo game on the page opposite.
- They will need two dice (numbered one to six) and twenty four counters.
- Children can take it in turns to be referee.
- The referee may want to use a multiplication table to check the answers. S/he should only check when both players have thought about the result of the multiplication.

Activities

Class game - preparation

- Provide a blank grid (with twelve squares) for each child.
- They should write any arrangement of numbers on their grid. **(Encourage them to think about possible products when the two dice are thrown, e.g. eleven would be a poor choice.)**
- Choose one child to be the caller and provide him/her with a multiplication table (up to and including the six times table), two dice (both numbered one to six) and a box of counters.

Playing the class game

For any number of players

- The caller shakes the dice and calls out the numbers.
- The caller records the throws by placing a counter on the appropriate place on the multiplication table, e.g. for five and three a counter should be place on fifteen:

×	1	2	3	4	5	6
1	1	2	3	4	5	6
2	2	4	6	8	10	12
3	3	6	9	12	●	18
4	4	8	12	16	20	24
5	5	10	15	20	25	30
6	6	12	18	24	30	36

- The players place a counter on their grid if they can.
- The winner is the first player to make a straight line with four counters.
- The caller can check their card with the counters on the multiplication table.

Variations

- The winner is the first player to complete the whole card.
- Use differently numbered dice, e.g. two to seven.

Display

The caller could use traditional bingo calling rhymes, e.g. legs eleven, all the fives fifty five, etc. Or they could invent their own, e.g. here comes Lee thirty three. The calls can be illustrated and displayed for further games:

The children could organise a Bingo game for other classes with prizes and display advertisement posters around the school.

Extension

- Investigate how many different scores are possible when two dice are thrown.
- Which scores can be obtained in more than one way? (E.g. 12 = 2 × 6, and 12 = 3 × 4.)
- Groups of children can devise, make and play their own Bingo games. They could make playing cards to use instead of dice, e.g:

3 × 8

© 1993 Folens Ltd.

Bingo

- This is a game for 2 players, A and B. C is the referee.
- A and B start by choosing a Bingo card.
- C throws 2 dice.
- Players multiply the dice scores, and place a counter on a square if it contains the result.
- If this cannot be done, do nothing.
- C checks both players' moves.
- The winner is the first player to make a straight line of 4 counters.

25	3	4	6
12	1	10	15
4	16	30	18

Player A

Player B

9	12	4	20
8	2	36	6
24	16	5	10

© 1993 Folens Ltd.   This page may be photocopied for classroom use only

Racing Cars - Ideas Page

Aim

- To explore division facts, leading towards understanding tests for divisibility.

Activity

Car race game - preparation

- Make a race course board (see below). The children may want to decorate the border with cheering crowds and advertisements.
- You will need ten cards from the activity page opposite and a dice numbered one to six.

Playing the car race game   *For one or more players*

- Place the cards at the start of the race.
- Throw the dice, then move forward one space, any car which is divisible by the dice number, e.g.

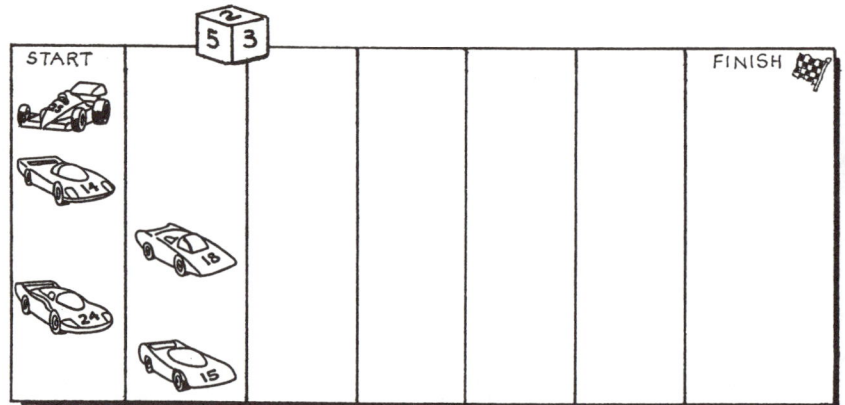

- Discuss which cars have most chance of winning.
- The players could each guess which one will win.

Activity page

The cards can be photocopied on to card, coloured and cut out. Laminate for longer life.

- Sort the cars into those which can and cannot be divided by two.
- Do the same for dividing by three, dividing by five, dividing by six, etc.
- Use the cards for the car race game.
- Take a copy of the page, white out the numbers, make some more cards, and invite the children to write some different numbers on the cards. These can then be added to the originals and sorted.

Display

Group the cars into 'cars divisible by two, three, four', etc. Ask the children to write about the patterns of the numbers. Display their work:

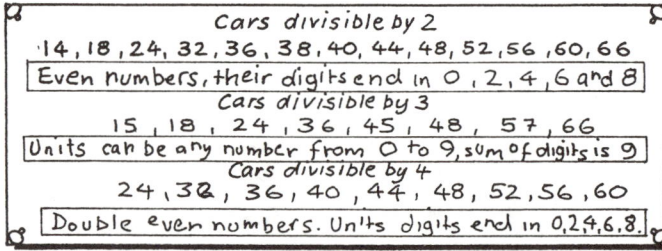

Extension

- Investigate cars which can be divided by two different numbers. E.g. cars divisible by two and three: eighteen, twenty four, thirty six, forty eight, sixty, sixty six.
- Which cars can be divided by three different numbers?
- Which numbered cars can only be divided by one and their own number (i.e. the prime numbers)?

© 1993 Folens Ltd.

Racing Cars

Cat, Rabbit or Koala - Ideas Page

Aim

- To provide experience in estimating the results of division, when two-digit and three-digit numbers are divided by single-digit numbers.

Activities

Activity page

- The answers:

Division	Guess			Answer
27 ÷ 3	5	10	15	9
52 ÷ 2	10	20	30	26
48 ÷ 4	10	15	20	12
84 ÷ 4	15	20	25	21
95 ÷ 5	10	20	30	19
126 ÷ 6	20	25	30	21
136 ÷ 2	60	80	100	68
207 ÷ 9	15	20	25	23

Mental mathematics

- Make a set of division flash cards, e.g:

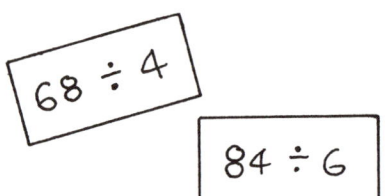

- Use card and laminate them for longer life.
- Present them to the children, one at a time.
- Ask the children to estimate them to the nearest ten or the nearest five.

Division estimating game *For two or three players*

- Each player takes it in turn to write down a division.
- Each player then makes a guess at the answer.
- The answer can be checked on a calculator.
- The player whose guess is nearest the correct answer wins.

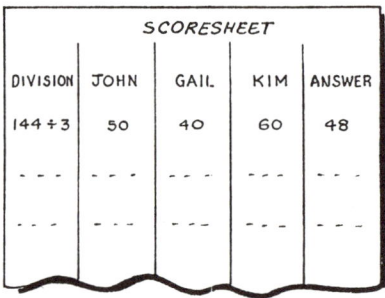

Extension

Division hat game *For two players*

- Place a set of numbered cards, one to nine in a hat.
- One player draws two cards, at random, from the hat, and orders them to make a two-digit number.
- The other player then throws a dice numbered one to six.
- The hat number has to be divided by the dice number.
- Each player estimates the size of the answer and writes it down.
- The answer can be checked on a calculator.
- The player who is the closest to the answer wins a point.
- The winner is the first player to gain five points.

© 1993 Folens Ltd.

Cat, Rabbit or Koala

- Look at the 3 possible answers to each division: Cat, Rabbit or Koala.
- Guess which one you think is the closest to the answer. Colour it.
- Then use a calculator to check and write down the actual answer.

Division	Guess	Answer
27 ÷ 3	5 10 15	
52 ÷ 2	10 20 30	
48 ÷ 4	10 15 20	
84 ÷ 4	15 20 25	
95 ÷ 5	10 20 30	
126 ÷ 6	20 25 30	
136 ÷ 2	60 80 100	
207 ÷ 9	15 20 25	

© 1993 Folens Ltd.

Multiplying by 9 - Ideas Page

Aims

- To explore the nine times table.
- To explore patterns related to the multiples of nine.

Mental mathematics

- Tell me a number between 120 and 130, which is a multiple of nine.
- What is the nearest multiple of nine to 116?
- I am thinking of a multiple of nine between one hundred and 200. If its units digit is four, what is the number?
- I am thinking of a two-digit multiple of nine. Which number could it be when the digit difference is five/one/three/two/four?
- Recite the multiples of nine forwards, starting at nine.
- Recite the multiples of nine backwards, starting at ninety nine.

Activities

Activity page

- Look at the patterns in the nine times table grid:

1	2	3	4	5	6	7	8	9	10
11	12	13	14	15	16	17	18	19	20
21	22	23	24	25	26	27	28	29	30
31	32	33	34	35	36	37	38	39	40
41	42	43	44	45	46	47	48	49	50
51	52	53	54	55	56	57	58	59	60
61	62	63	64	65	66	67	68	69	70
71	72	73	74	75	76	77	78	79	80
81	82	83	84	85	86	87	88	89	90
91	92	93	94	95	96	97	98	99	100

- The multiples of nine form a diagonal line in the one to one hundred counting square.
- Note the increasing sequence in the tens digit and the decreasing sequence in the units digit.
- Note that the sum of the digits of each multiple is nine.

- Are these patterns true for multiples of nine which are greater than ninety? If not, what happens?
- How can you tell, quickly, if a number is divisible by nine?

- Extend the table to 200.
- Note that eighteen and eighty one are multiples of nine, and one is the reverse of the other. Also, 18 + 81 = 100.
- Investigate similar patterns in the other multiples of nine. Extend to, for example, 126 and 621.
- Explore the digit sums of multiples of other numbers.

Display

Ask the children to make a set of cards numbered one to nine. They should select three of the cards to make a three-digit number which is a multiple of nine. (This can be checked on the calculator.)
In pairs children can explore how many different three-digit numbers can be created with them, e.g:

| 3 | 1 | 5 | | 5 | 1 | 3 | | 5 | 3 | 1 |

| 1 | 3 | 5 | | 1 | 5 | 3 | | 3 | 5 | 1 |

Using a calculator, they can then investigate whether they are all multiples of nine and write about why they think this is.

Display the children's written work below their numbered cards.

Extension

- List all the multiples of nine between 500 and 600. How many are there?
- In pairs, the children can practise using their fingers to multiply by nine, as explained opposite.

E.g. **9 x 4 =**

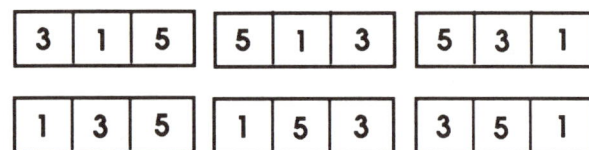

36

Multiplying by 9

Colour the multiples of 9 in the grid. Then complete the chart.

1	2	3	4	5	6	7	8	9	10
11	12	13	14	15	16	17	18	19	20
21	22	23	24	25	26	27	28	29	30
31	32	33	34	35	36	37	38	39	40
41	42	43	44	45	46	47	48	49	50
51	52	53	54	55	56	57	58	59	60
61	62	63	64	65	66	67	68	69	70
71	72	73	74	75	76	77	78	79	80
81	82	83	84	85	86	87	88	89	90
91	92	93	94	95	96	97	98	99	100

Multiples of 9	Digit sum
9	
18	
27	2 + 7 = 9
36	

Use your fingers to multiply by 9. Spread your fingers and thumbs, imagining they are numbered like this.

To multiply 9 by 4. Bend the 4th finger.

Then count the fingers to the left ⟵ 3 and right 6 ⟶

The result is  36

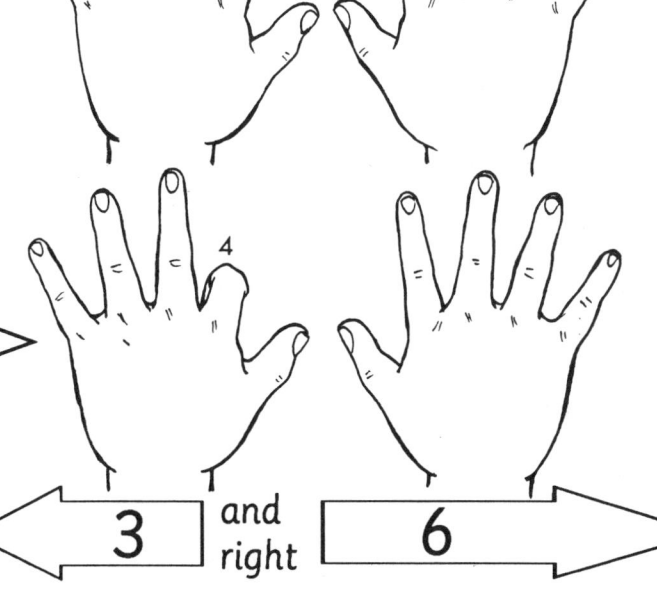

Hundred Game - Ideas Page

Aims

- To practise multiplying two single-digit numbers.
- To practise adding two-digit numbers.

Mental mathematics

Throw two dice and call out:
- the score asking the children for the product
- the product asking the children for the two dice scores.

- Call out the two dice scores, asking the children to multiply the total by seven. (Extend this to multiplying by other numbers.)
- Call out the two dice scores asking the children to multiply, e.g. five by the dice difference.

Activities

Activity page

- There are many ways of achieving exactly one hundred in three throws:

all three different	one throw repeated
32, 48, 20	35, 35, 30
32, 28, 40	40, 40, 20
35, 25, 40	30, 30, 40
16, 36, 48	42, 42, 16
24, 28, 48	36, 36, 28

Variations of the hundred game

- Increase the target from one hundred to 200.
- Play the game by starting with a total of 200 and subtracting the score each time. The winner is the first player to reach nought or below.
- Change the numbering on the dice. (A simpler version uses two dice numbered one to six. A harder version uses one dice numbered four to six and one numbered three to eight.)
- Use a shuffled pack of playing cards (without picture cards). The players can generate the two numbers to be multiplied by taking turns to reveal the top two cards in the pile.

Display

Display the children's art/design and written work.

Creative writing

Ask the children to imagine they are a dice with six faces. They could describe their shape, colour and each face. Do they have a favourite face? Do they dislike one of their faces? How are they used in a game?

Art/design

Ask the children to design a net to make a cube.

They could design numerals or other ways of marking the faces.

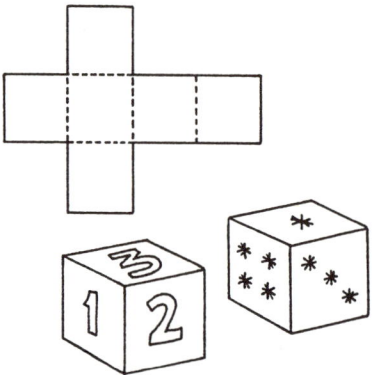

Extension

- Draw a multiplication table to show the possible results of one throw scores using different types of dice, e.g. using dice numbered one to six and three to eight:

X	1	2	3	4	5	6
3	3	6	9	12	15	18
4	4	8	12	16	20	24
5	5	10	15	20	25	30
6	6	12	18	24	30	36
7	7	14	21	28	35	42
8	8	16	24	32	40	48

© 1993 Folens Ltd.

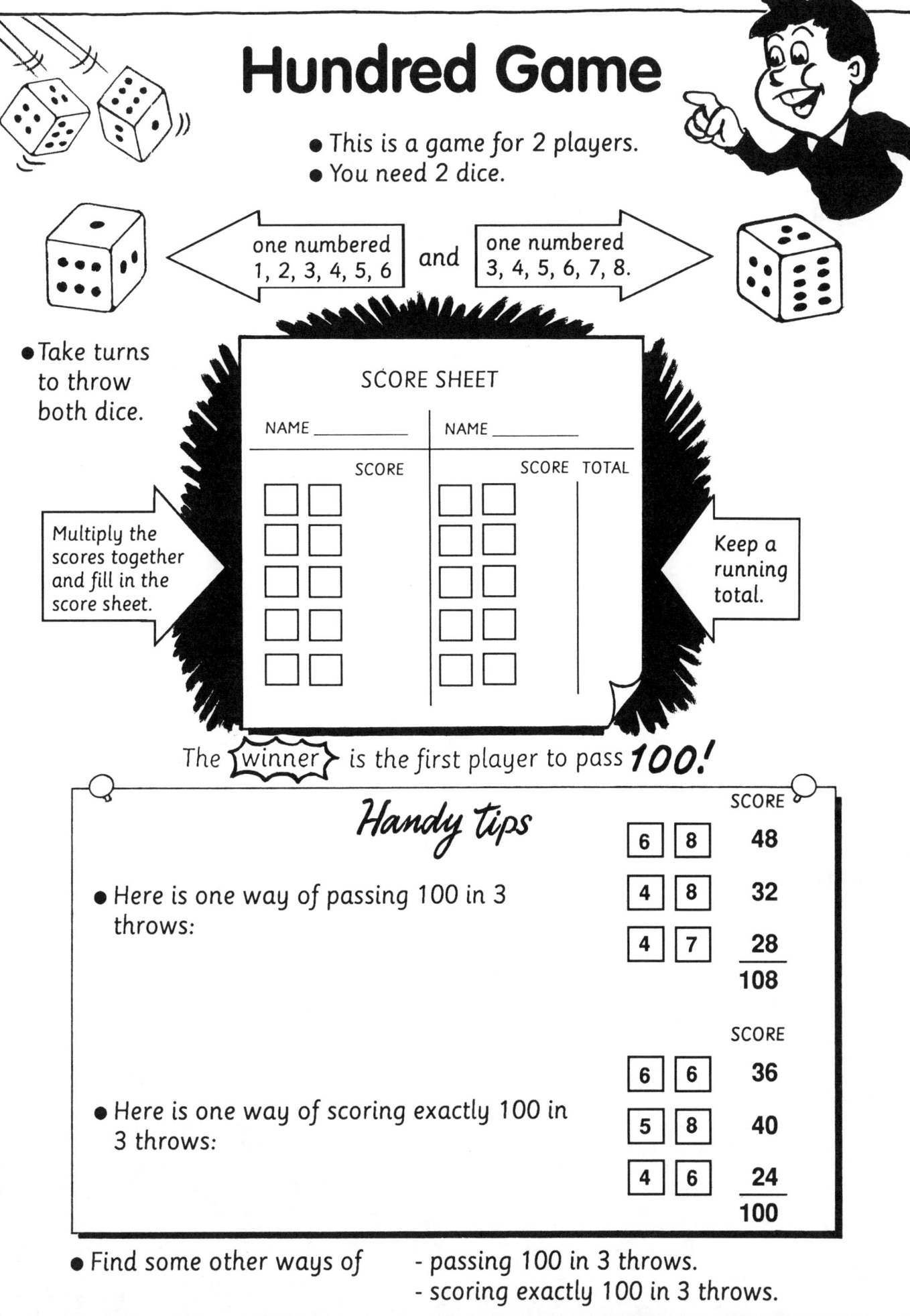

Remainder Athletics - Ideas Page

Aim

- To explore patterns in the remainders when dividing by a single-digit number.

Mental mathematics

- What number am I?
  I am between twenty and thirty.
  I give a remainder of three when divided by seven.
- Name five numbers which give a remainder of one when divided by three.

Twenty to thirty

- Consider numbers between twenty and thirty.
- Which numbers give the highest remainder when they are divided by six, seven, eight, etc?

Activities

Activity page

- The answers:

The **blue** team	4, 8, 12, 16, 20
The **red** team	1, 5, 9, 13, 17
The **yellow** team	2, 6, 10, 14, 18
The **green** team	3, 7, 11, 15, 19

- Note that blue and yellow are always even, red and green are always odd.

- When dividing by five, there will be five teams:

exactly divisible by 5	5, 10, 15, 20
remainder 1	1, 6, 11, 16
remainder 2	2, 7, 12, 17
remainder 3	3, 8, 13, 18
reminder 4	4, 9, 14, 19

- Note the patterns in the units digit of each team.

Extension

The remainder game   *For two or more players*

- Each player should make a remainder board with thirty six squares. The squares should have a number between nought and seven written inside them.
- Each player takes it in turn to throw two dice.
- All players multiply the dice scores together, and divide the result by seven. They can place a counter on a number on their own board which matches the remainder.
- The winner is the first player to have four counters in a straight line.

© 1993 Folens Ltd.

Remainder Athletics

- In Remainder Athletics there are 4 teams - blue, red, yellow and green.
- To find out the teams, divide by 4.
- The Blue team has numbers which divide exactly by 4. Colour their kit blue.
- Colour the other teams:
  - red has numbers which give a remainder of 1
  - yellow has numbers which give a remainder of 2
  - green numbers give a remainder of 3.

- Which other numbers could belong to each team?
- Find out the teams if you divide by 5.

The Factor Tribe - Ideas Page

Aims

- To consider the pairs of possible factors of different numbers.
- To consolidate ideas associated with prime numbers.

Mental mathematics

- I am thinking of a three-legged member of the tribe. One of his boots is 2 × 10, what are the other two?

New tribes

- Invent different tribes. The tribes can be distinguished by:
  - division facts
  - addition facts
  - subtraction facts
  - number of factors.

Activities

Activity page

- The boot facts are:

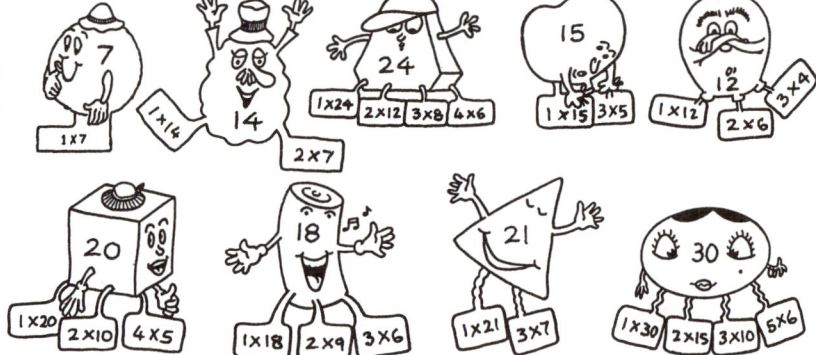

- If the tribe has fifty members (labelled one to fifty) how many of each type are there?

One-legged members	1, 2, 3, 5, 7, 11, 13, 17, 19, 23, 29, 31, 37, 41, 43, 47
Two-legged members	4, 6, 8, 9, 10, 14, 15, 21, 22, 25, 26, 27, 33, 34, 35, 38, 39, 44, 46, 49, 50
Three-legged members	12, 16, 18, 20, 28, 32, 45
Four-legged members	24, 30, 40, 42
Five-legged members	36, 48

- Extend to numbers fifty to one hundred.
- Investigate odd and even numbers.

Display

Sections can be devoted to displaying one-legged members, two-legged members, etc.
They can be represented by sticky circles, coloured red for one leg, green for two legs, and so on ...

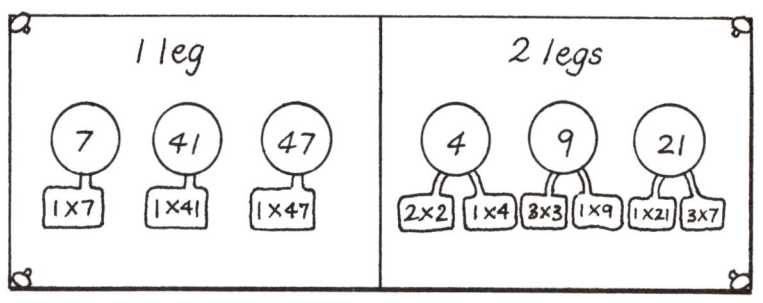

Extension

- Invite pupils to make sets of boots on card, each card containing a different table fact.
- These can be used for different activities, e.g. a sorting activity: sort them into sets to see which boots belong to each tribe member.

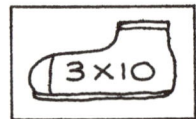

© 1993 Folens Ltd.

The Factor Tribe

- Meet the factor tribe, each one is a different number.
  Some are 1-legged, some 2-legged, some have more than 2 legs.
  They have different table facts written on their boots, to match their number.
- Complete the table facts on their boots.

- Draw some more members of the factor tribe.
- Sort them into 1-legged, 2-legged, 3-legged, and so on.

Make it Big - Ideas Page

Aims

- To consider the postioning of digits in multiplications involving:
  - two-digit number x single-digit number
  - two-digit number x two-digit number
  - three-digit number x two-digit number.

Activities

Activity page

- The arrangements for maximum products are:

```
   3 2        5 2        5 4 2
 x   4      x 4 3      x   6 3
 ─────      ─────      ───────
 1 2 8      2 2 3 6    3 4 1 4 6
```

- If a, b, c and d are in ascending order, then the maximum product is:

```
   b a        d a        d c a
 x   c      x c b      x   e b
```

- Pupils could make a set of numbered cards for each activity.
- The calculator is necessary, so that the focus of the activity is on the arrangement of the digits.

Display

Display four numbered cards. Ask groups of children to arrange the numbers into different multiplication sums. They can then stick their sums on to the wall underneath the cards, e.g:

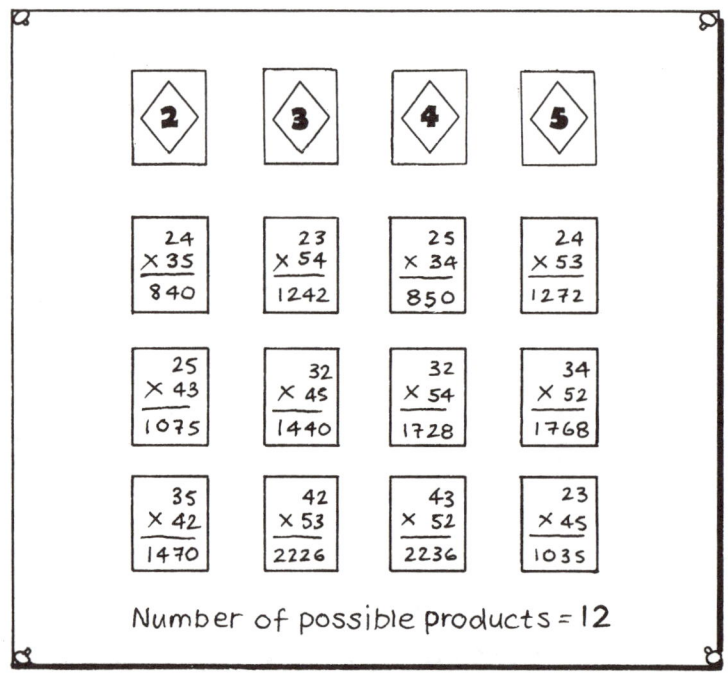

Extension

- Investigate arrangements to give the smallest possible product.
- Try the same multiplications using a different set of digits.
- Extend to division problems, i.e:

© 1993 Folens Ltd.

Make it Big!

Use a calculator to help you.
In each multiplication you are only allowed to use a given set of digits.
Find out which arrangement gives the largest possible answer.

- Use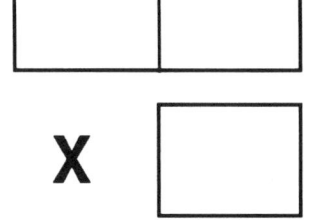

- Use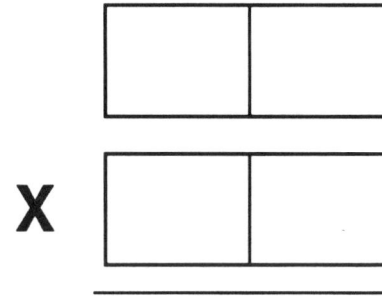

- Use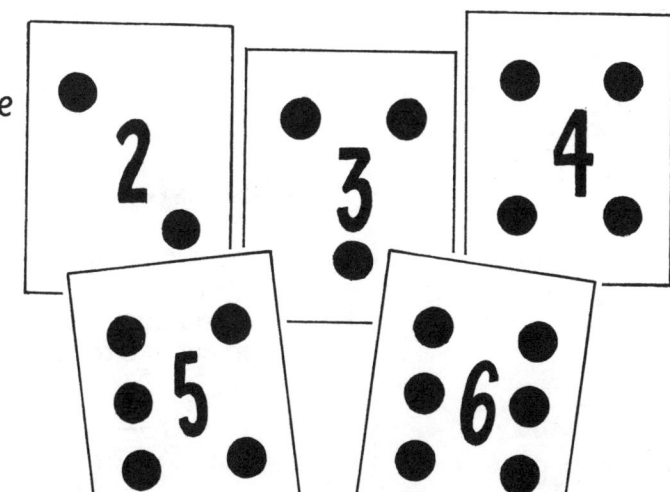

Number Machine - Ideas Page

Aims

- To consolidate the learning of multiplication tables via the concept of a function machine.
- To understand that division is the inverse of multiplication.

Activities

Activity page

- Make a set of 'Multiply by' labels, e.g:

| MULTIPLY BY 4 | MULTIPLY BY 9 | MULTIPLY BY 7 |

... and a set of 'Divide by' labels, e.g:

| DIVIDE BY 2 | DIVIDE BY 5 | DIVIDE BY 6 |

- You also need a set of cards or discs numbered from one to ten:

... and a set of product cards or discs:

    . . .

- Photocopy the number machine opposite.

Using the machine

- Place a 'multiply by' or 'divide by' label on to the middle section of the machine.
- Use the numbered cards (one to ten) to feed the machine, and the product discs to record the answer.

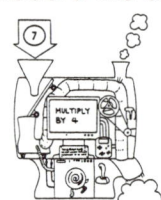

Stage 1

- Explore the product of feeding different numbers into the 'multiply by' machines:

Stage 2

- Explore the reverse, i.e. which number needs to be fed into the machine to produce a given product?

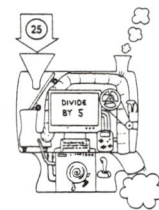

Stage 3

- Explore, in the same way 'divide by' machines:

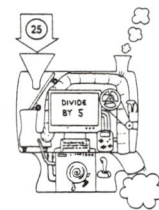

Display

Display pictures of different machines on the wall. Change them each day, by varying the labels on the machines.

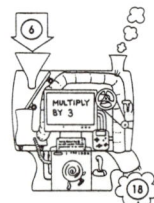 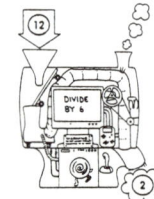 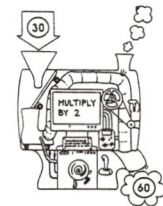

Extension

- Introduce a 'Multiply together' label, for which two numbers have to be fed into the machine.

© 1993 Folens Ltd.

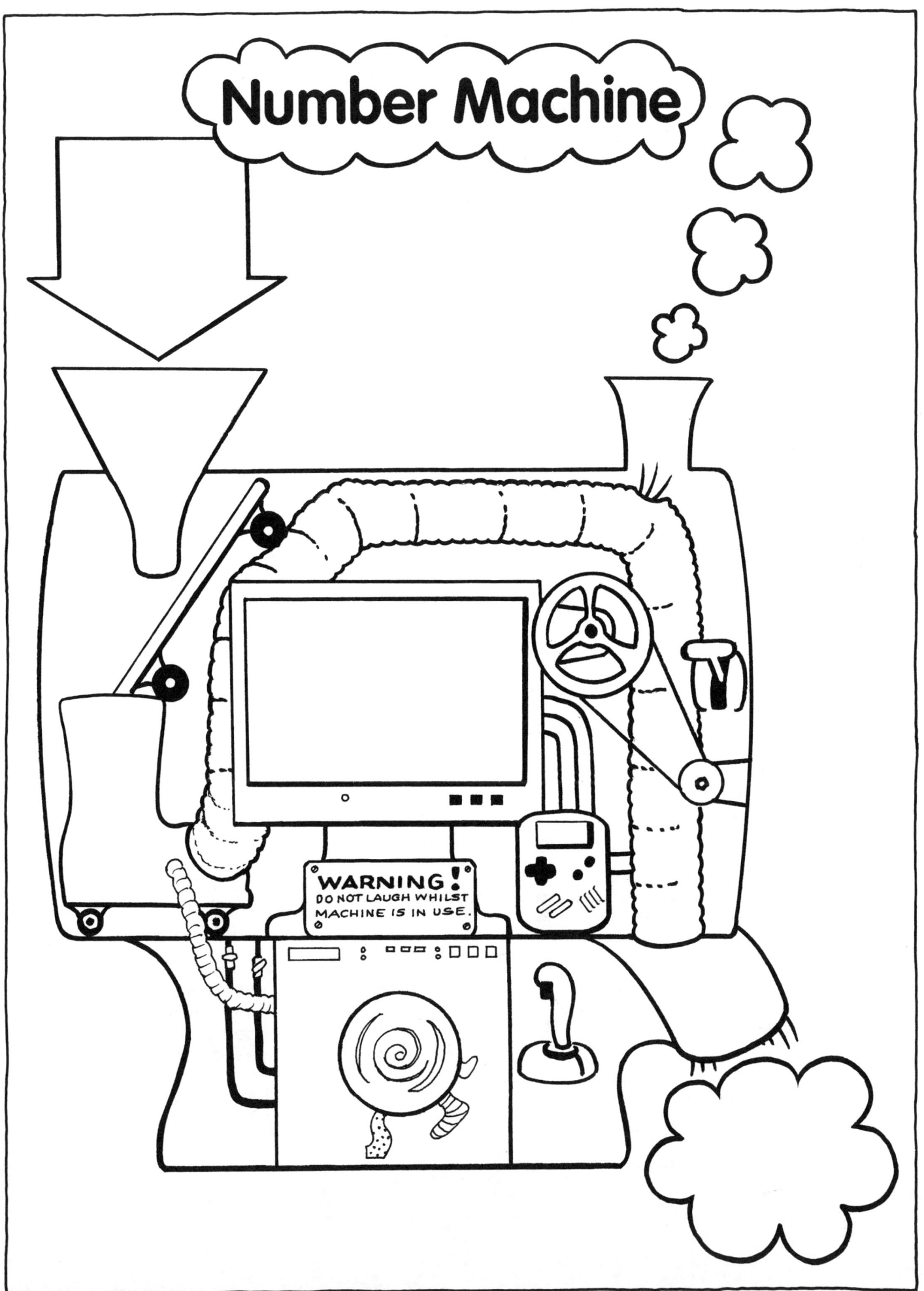

Prime Time - Ideas Page

Aim

- To explore prime numbers, and patterns associated with them.

The *Sieve of Eratosthenes*

The activity demonstrates a method for producing prime numbers. It is known as the *Sieve of Eratosthenes*.
- The numbers with no markings are the prime numbers, i.e. they are not divisible by any number except themselves.
- It is interesting to see that, apart from two and three, the prime numbers fall into two columns, illustrating that they are always either one more or one less than a multiple of six.

Activities

Activity page

- The result of the activity is:

1	2	3	④	5	⬡6⬡
7	⑧	▢9▢	⑩△	11	▢12▢
13	⨯14⨯	△15△	⑯	17	▢18▢
19	⑳	⨯21⨯	㉒	23	▢24▢
△25△	㉖	27	⨯28⨯	29	㉚△
31	㉜	33	㉞	⨯35⨯	▢36▢
37	㊳	39	㊵△	41	▢42▢⨯
43	㊹	△45△	㊻	47	▢48▢
⨯49⨯	㊿	51	㊾	53	▢54▢
△55△	⨯56⨯	57	㊿	59	▢60▢△

- Discuss the numbers which have been both circled and squared (multiples of six), both circled and triangled (multiples of ten), both squared and triangled (multiples of fifteen), etc.
- Which numbers have three markings? (E.g. forty two has been circled, triangled and crossed.)

Display

As a result of the activity, and extending it, display a list of the prime numbers:

```
            PRIME NUMBERS
         11      31  41      61  71        101
  2  3   13  23      43  53      73  83    103
  5  7   17      37  47      67          97 107
         19  29              59      79  89 109
```

Mark the primes on a number line:

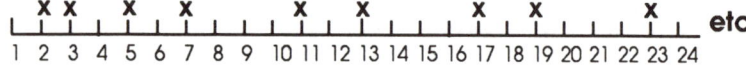

Extension

- Extend the table to one hundred or even 200, and find the prime numbers greater than sixty.
- There will need to be additional sifting, e.g. the next elimination is to delete all multiples of eleven except eleven, then all multiples of thirteen except thirteen.
- Alternatively try the activity on a one to one hundred counting square.

Prime Time

- Circle the multiples of 2, except 2   ○
- Square the multiples of 3, except 3   □
- Triangle the multiples of 5, except 5   △
- Cross the multiples of 7, except 7   ✗

1	2	3	4	5	6
7	8	9	10	11	12
13	14	15	16	17	18
19	20	21	22	23	24
25	26	27	28	29	30
31	32	33	34	35	36
37	38	39	40	41	42
43	44	45	46	47	48
49	50	51	52	53	54
55	56	57	58	59	60

Multiple Cards - Ideas Page

Aim

- To explore the multiples of different numbers.

Activities

Activity page

The cards can be photocopied on to card, coloured and then cut out. Laminate them for longer life. They can be used many times for a variety of different activities.

- Possible solutions can be found by looking along the rows of a multiplication square:

1	2	3	4	5	6	7	8	9	10
2	4	6	8	10	12	14	16	18	20
3	6	9	12	15	18	21	24	27	30
4	8	12	16	20	24	28	32	36	40
5	10	15	20	25	30	35	40	45	50
6	12	18	24	30	36	42	48	54	60
7	14	21	28	35	42	49	56	63	70
8	16	24	32	40	48	56	64	72	80
9	18	27	36	45	54	63	72	81	90
10	20	30	40	50	60	70	80	90	100

- Other solutions exist if the rows and columns are extended.

Multiple hat game
For two or three players

- Use the activity cards opposite.
- Provide each player with a multiplication square.
- Place all the cards into a hat.
- Each player takes it in turn to draw out two cards and arrange them to make a two-digit number.
- Each player needs to work out whether their number is a multiple of any of the numbers on the multiplication squares. They can colour in the appropriate numbers.
- The winner is the first one to colour in a line of six numbers horizontally, vertically or diagonally.

Display

Present the children with a challenge. Ask them to use the cards to make different multiples of four using each card only once. When the children have completed the challenge, display their results:

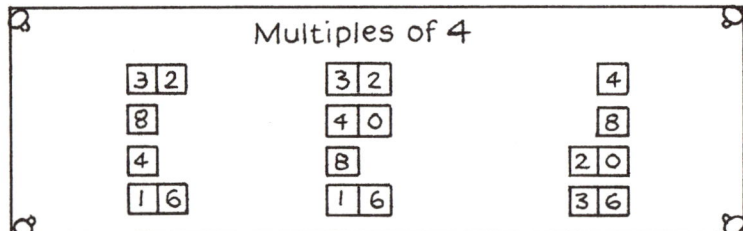

Note. It is possible to show four different multiples of four in several different ways (as above).

Extension

- Try to use all the cards to make five different two-digit multiples, e.g.

x3	x6	x9
12	18	18
39	30	27
45	54	36
60	72	45
78	96	90

© 1993 Folens Ltd.

Homework Marking - Ideas Page

Aim

- To provide reinforcement of:
  - dividing two-digit numbers by a single-digit number.
  - multiplying a two-digit number by a single-digit number.

- Invite the children to provide correct solutions to each of the six 'wrong answers'.

Activities

Activity page

- There are six errors in the homework, giving a correct mark of fourteen out of twenty.
- The corrected answers are ringed below:

4. $3\overline{)28}$ = ⑨ rem 1

5. $6\overline{)39}$ = 6 rem ③

11. $3\overline{)23}$ = 7 rem ②

14. $\begin{array}{r} 23 \\ \times 2 \\ \hline ④6 \end{array}$

16. $\begin{array}{r} 18 \\ \times 4 \\ \hline 7② \end{array}$

18. $\begin{array}{r} 19 \\ \times 7 \\ \hline 13③ \end{array}$

Extension

Preparing homework

- Ask the children to write down the solutions to these ten division problems, but include three errors.

1. 15 ÷ 2   2. 22 ÷ 3   3. 19 ÷ 4   4. 28 ÷ 5

5. 36 ÷ 6   6. 29 ÷ 7   7. 61 ÷ 8   8. 48 ÷ 9

9. 54 ÷ 10   10. 83 ÷ 11

- On the back of the paper they should write down corrections to the errors.
- Invite pupils to set a ten question homework.
- It must be based on a specific aspect of mathematics, e.g.
  - long multiplication
  - addition of two-digit numbers
  - subtraction of one two-digit number from another.
- The homework must be neatly presented, together with a page of correct solutions and a marking scheme.
- Appropriate homeworks can be selected and given to other children.

© 1993 Folens Ltd.

Homework Marking

This is Janice's homework. How did she do?
Tick the correct answers, awarding 1 mark for each question.
Circle the errors.
Give a mark out of 20.

1. 4)38 = 9 remainder 2

2. 5)52 = 10 remainder 2

3. 7)36 = 5 remainder 1

4. 3)28 = 8 remainder 1

5. 6)39 = 6 remainder 5

6. 9)31 = 3 remainder 4

7. 2)19 = 9 remainder 1

8. 8)63 = 7 remainder 7

9. 10)74 = 7 remainder 4

10. 5)28 = 5 remainder 3

11. 3)23 = 7 remainder 1

12. 4)29 = 7 remainder 1

13. 35 × 4 = 140

14. 23 × 2 = 56

15. 32 × 5 = 160

16. 18 × 4 = 76

17. 13 × 9 = 117

18. 19 × 7 = 134

19. 44 × 2 = 88

20. 23 × 6 = 138

© 1993 Folens Ltd.

Line Graphs - Ideas Page

Aims

- To practise the learning of multiplication facts.
- To explore patterns in the units digits of the multiples.

Mental mathematics

- What is the pattern of the end digits for the five times table?
- Recite the five times table.
- What is the pattern in the end digits for the ten times table?
- Recite the ten times table.
- Pose the same tasks and questions for other multiplication tables. The patterns should help children to recite the tables.
  Consider, e.g. the four times table graph:
  - which bottom number is joined by a top number of three, of five, etc?

Activities

Activity page

- The completed charts should look like this:

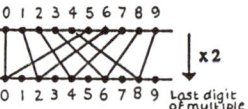 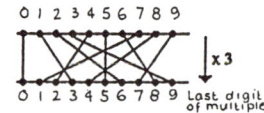 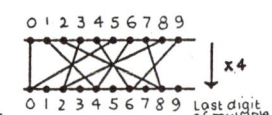
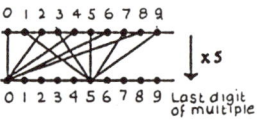 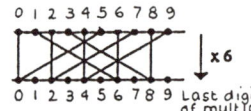 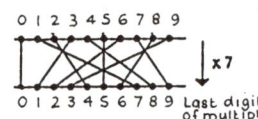
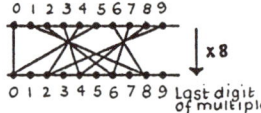 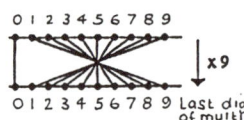 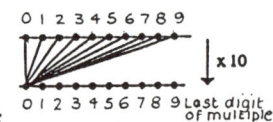

- Discuss the patterns in the charts.
- Note that:
  - some multiples only map to one end digit (x10)
  - some map to two end digits (x5)
  - some map to five end digits (x2, x4, x6, x8)
  - some map to all end digits (x3, x7, x9)
- Look at the special pattern in x9.
- Further charts can be drawn using squared paper to mark the divisions.

Display

Concentrate on two multiplication tables at a time, e.g. five and ten. Display the completed charts for these tables next to a large multiplication table:

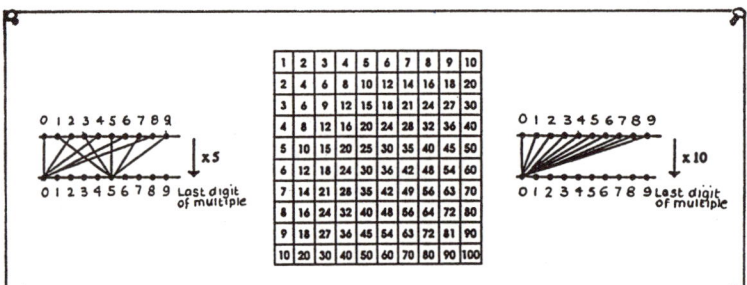

Circle the end digits for the selected tables. The displays can then be used for discussion and number pattern investigation.

Extension

- Explore the patterns in the sequences of the end digits, e.g.

x2	2 4	4 6	6 8	8 0	0 2	2 4
x3	3 1	6 4	9 7	2 0	5 3	8 6
x4	4 8	8 2	2 6	6 0	0 4	4 8
x5	5 5	0 0	5 5	0 0	5 5	0 0

© 1993 Folens Ltd.

Line Graphs

Make a multiplication line graph.

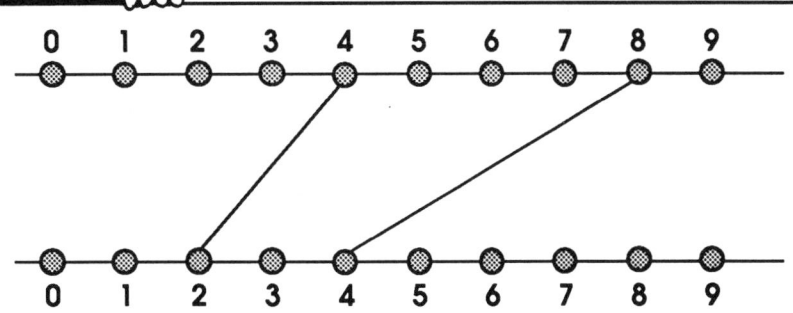

Last digit of multiple

1 Multiply the numbers on the top line by 3.
2 Join a line to the last digit of the product.

Examples: **4 x 3 = 12** so join **4 to 2**

  8 x 3 = 24 so join **8 to 4**

• Complete the graph by drawing the other lines.

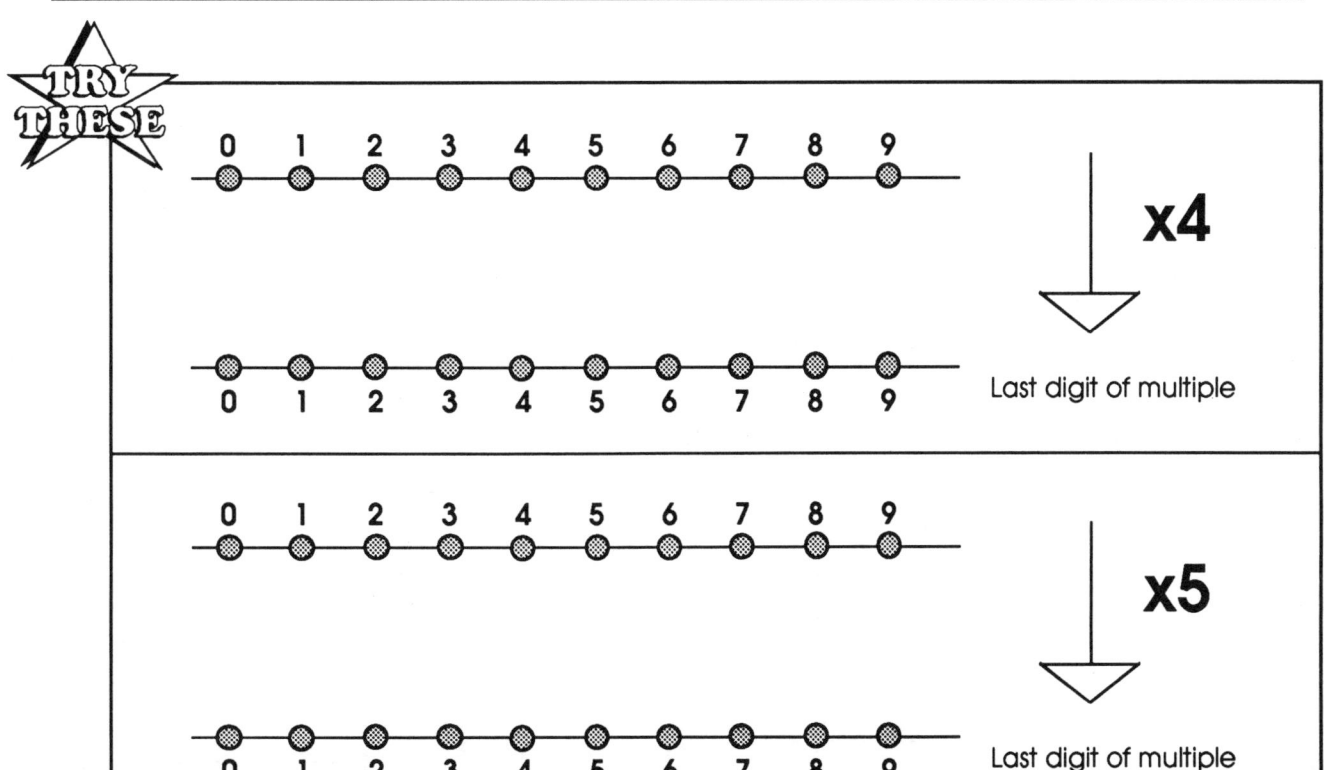

• Draw the line graphs for some other multiples.

Calculator Division - Ideas Page

Aim

- To create division facts, when limited to a set of given digits.

Investigation

- What is the largest and smallest possible result when dividing by three, dividing by four, and so on.
- Choose a different set of five digits to explore different divisions.

Activities

Activity page

- A sticky square or symbol could be placed on top of the keys which are not to be used.
- After an initial trial and error exploration, the children should begin to use a systematic strategy, i.e. take a particular digit and consider possible division facts when dividing by that digit.
E.g.

$$46 \div 2 = 23$$

- is four divisible by two? Yes.
- is six also divisible by two? Yes.
- therefore forty six will be divisible by two.

Display

Different facts can be displayed as they are found:

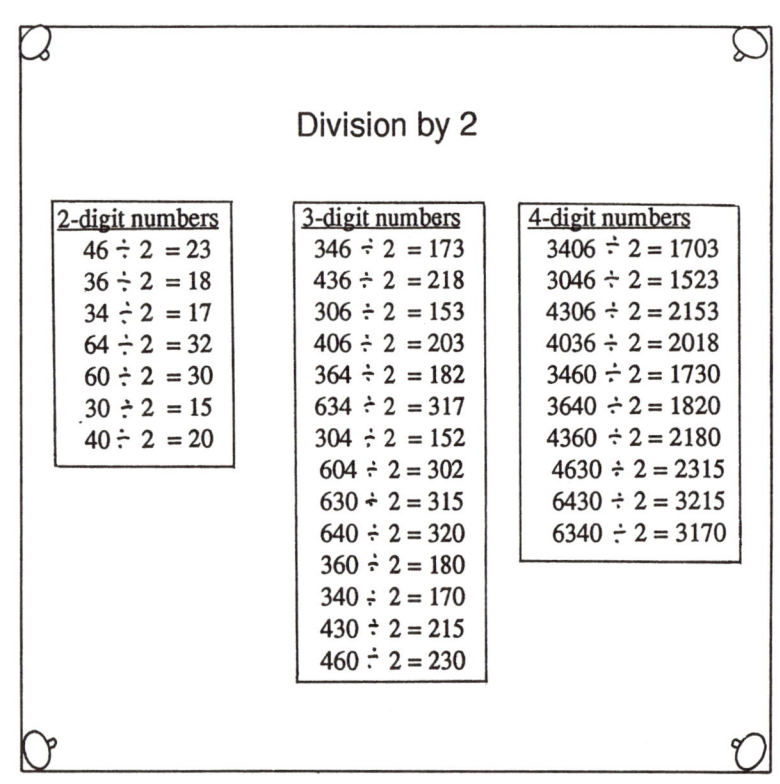

Division by 2

2-digit numbers	3-digit numbers	4-digit numbers
46 ÷ 2 = 23	346 ÷ 2 = 173	3406 ÷ 2 = 1703
36 ÷ 2 = 18	436 ÷ 2 = 218	3046 ÷ 2 = 1523
34 ÷ 2 = 17	306 ÷ 2 = 153	4306 ÷ 2 = 2153
64 ÷ 2 = 32	406 ÷ 2 = 203	4036 ÷ 2 = 2018
60 ÷ 2 = 30	364 ÷ 2 = 182	3460 ÷ 2 = 1730
30 ÷ 2 = 15	634 ÷ 2 = 317	3640 ÷ 2 = 1820
40 ÷ 2 = 20	304 ÷ 2 = 152	4360 ÷ 2 = 2180
	604 ÷ 2 = 302	4630 ÷ 2 = 2315
	630 ÷ 2 = 315	6430 ÷ 2 = 3215
	640 ÷ 2 = 320	6340 ÷ 2 = 3170
	360 ÷ 2 = 180	
	340 ÷ 2 = 170	
	430 ÷ 2 = 215	
	460 ÷ 2 = 230	

Extension

Investigation

- The children could make a set of cards ...

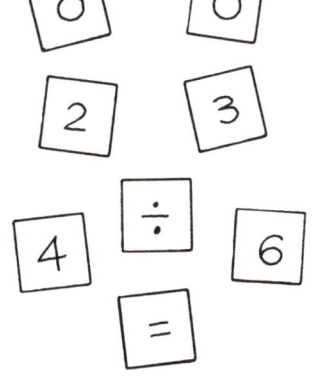

... and manipulate them to help seek different solutions:

| 4 | 6 | ÷ | 2 | = | 2 | 3 |

| 1 | 2 | ÷ | 2 | = | 6 |

Calculator Division

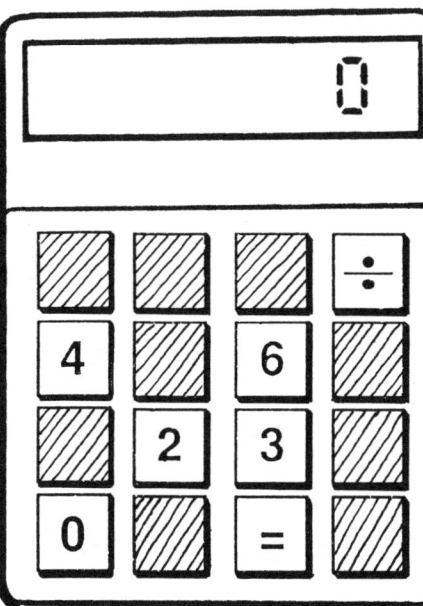

- Use a calculator.
- You may only use the keys shown.
- The other keys must not be pressed.
- So, you have the number keys:

| 0 | 2 | 3 | 4 | 6 |

... and the symbol keys:

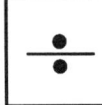

- Create divisions which give exact answers.

  Examples:

  | 4 | 6 | ÷ | 2 | = | 23

  | 6 | 0 | ÷ | 3 | = | 20

- How many more can you find?

- Change to a different set of 5 number keys and see how many exact divisions you can create.

Eight ways to help ...

There are hundreds of ideas in this book to enable you to develop and extend the photocopiable pages. Here are just eight ways to help you make the most of the Ideas Bank series.

1 Photocopy a page, paste on to card and laminate/cover with sticky backed plastic to use with groups. Children can now write on the pages using water-based pens and this can be washed off.

2 Photocopy on to both sides of the paper. Put another useful activity on the back. Develop a simple filing system so others can find relevant sheets and do not duplicate them again.

3 Save the sheets - if the children do not have to cut them up as a part of the activity - and re-use. Label the sets, and keep them safely in files.

4 Make the most of group work. Children working in small groups only need one sheet to discuss between them.

5 Put the sheets inside clear plastic wallets. This means the sheets are easily stored in a binder and will last longer. Children's writing can again be wiped away.

6 Use as an ideas page for yourself. Discuss issues with the class and get children to produce artwork and writing.

7 Make an overhead transparency of the page. You and your colleagues can now use the idea time and time again.

8 Ask yourself: "Does every child in this class/group need to deal with/work through this photocopiable sheet?" If not, don't photocopy it!

© 1993 Folens Ltd.